COPING WITH WORKPLACE CHANGE
Dealing with Loss and Grief

WITHDRAWN

J. Shep Jeffreys, Ed.D.

A FIFTY-MINUTE™ SERIES BOOK

CRISP PUBLICATIONS, INC.
Menlo Park, California

COPING WITH WORKPLACE CHANGE
Dealing with Loss and Grief

J. Shep Jeffreys, Ed.D.

CREDITS
Managing Editor: **Kathleen Barcos**
Editor: **Carol Henry**
Typesetting: **ExecuStaff**
Cover Design: **Carol Harris**
Artwork: **Ralph Mapson**

All rights reserved. No part of this book may be reproduced or transmitted in any form or by any means now known or to be invented, electronic or mechanical, including photocopying, recording, or by any information storage or retrieval system without written permission from the author or publisher, except for the brief inclusion of quotations in a review.

Copyright © 1995 by Crisp Publications, Inc.

Printed in the United States of America by Bawden Printing Company.

English language Crisp books are distributed worldwide. Our major international distributors include:

CANADA: Reid Publishing Ltd., Box 69559—109 Thomas St., Oakville, Ontario, Canada L6J 7R4. TEL: (905) 842-4428, FAX: (905) 842-9327

Raincoast Books Distribution Ltd., 112 East 3rd Avenue, Vancouver, British Columbia, Canada V5T 1C8. TEL: (604) 873-6581, FAX: (604) 874-2711

AUSTRALIA: Career Builders, P.O. Box 1051, Springwood, Brisbane, Queensland, Australia 4127. TEL: 841-1061, FAX: 841-1580

NEW ZEALAND: Career Builders, P.O. Box 571, Manurewa, Auckland, New Zealand. TEL: 266-5276, FAX: 266-4152

JAPAN: Phoenix Associates Co., Mizuho Bldg. 2-12-2, Kami Osaki, Shinagawa-Ku, Tokyo 141, Japan. TEL: 3-443-7231, FAX: 3-443-7640

Selected Crisp titles are also available in other languages. Contact International Rights Manager Suzanne Kelly at (415) 323-6100 for more information.

Library of Congress Catalog Card Number 94-68197
Jeffreys, J. Shep
Coping with Workplace Change
ISBN 1-56052-308-5

This book is printed on recyclable paper with soy ink.

ABOUT THIS BOOK

Coping with Workplace Change is not like most books. It has a unique "self-study" format that encourages a reader to become personally involved. Designed to be "read with a pencil," the book offers an abundance of exercises, activities, assessments and cases that invite participation.

This book introduces you to concepts about grief in the workplace and teaches specific skills in helping yourself and others. It further recommends activities and programs for organizations to use during times of workplace change, loss and grief.

Coping with Workplace Change can be used effectively in a number of ways. Here are some possibilities:

—Individual Study. Because the book is self-instructional, all that is needed is a quiet place, some time and a pencil. By completing the activities and exercises, a reader should not only receive valuable feedback, but also take practical steps in helping employees successfully manage the process of workplace loss and change.

—Workshops and Seminars. This book is ideal for reading prior to a workshop or seminar. With the basics in hand, the quality of participation will improve. More time can be spent in concept extensions and applications during the program. The book is also effective when a trainer distributes it at the beginning of a session and leads participants through the contents.

There are other possibilities that depend on the objectives, program or ideas of the user. One thing is certain: even after it has been read, this book will serve as excellent reference material that can be easily reviewed.

ABOUT THE AUTHOR

Dr. John Shep Jeffreys is a Columbia, Maryland-based psychologist with a general family practice and a specialty in the treatment of grief-related problems. He also consults with medical, educational and business organizations concerning issues of change, loss and grief.

His consulting practice, John S. Jeffreys, Ed.D. & Associates, provides on-site training and public seminars for personnel and consultants who assist organizations in coping with change, loss and grief, as well as retreats and individual coaching for executives on workplace grief.

Dr. Jeffreys has worked as a trainer and workshop leader with Elisabeth Kübler-Ross, M.D. He is an instructor in Psychiatry at Johns Hopkins University School of Medicine.

Dr. Jeffreys is President of the Steven Daniel Jeffreys Foundation, Ltd., a nonprofit organization dedicated to serving people in grief over life's losses. The Foundation was created by Dr. Jeffreys' family in memory of his son Steven, who died at age eight in 1975.

PREFACE

"The sound of change is growing louder."

—Ivory Dorsey
National Speakers Association
Convention, 1994

Dear Reader:

Reading this book may be your first step in taking control of a painful time in your life, or in advising others whom you are in a position to help.

This book is designed for helping yourself and others to understand grief and do something about it. It is an interactive book, and I'm asking you in advance to *do all of the exercises* so you will get the most benefit from the reading selections.

We don't always have much influence over the losses that life hands us. What we *can* control is how we respond to change, loss and grief. This book will provide you with a strong beginning to taking control of workplace grief.

Anyone who has grieved or has been concerned about the grief of others will never again see grief as weak or unnecessary. After reading this book, grief will never quite be the same for you or your co-workers.

You will be learning the following concepts and skills:

- Why we are experiencing so much change in the workplace

- How change in the workplace becomes loss and grief in the workplace

- Why workplace attachments are the basis for employee loss and grief

- The normal feelings, attitudes and behaviors of grief reaction

- How grief reaction affects employee productivity

- How employee grief moves through predictable stages and phases

- The Four Tasks of mourning that must be accomplished in order to heal grief

- How to help employees accomplish the Four Tasks

PREFACE (continued)

- How to listen helpfully to grieving employees

- Additional specific suggestions for helping grieving employees

- How to recognize when an employee needs specialized help

- How organizations can provide programs to help grieving employees

My best wishes.

J. Shep Jeffreys, Ed.D.

CONTENTS

ACKNOWLEDGMENTS

No undertaking such as this book happens without very special help from others.

First, I acknowledge my teacher, Elisabeth Kübler-Ross, M.D., who has enabled me to travel my own path of grief to healing and service to others.

Special thanks to Richard Yocum, Chairman of The Executive Committee, for a detailed review of the manuscript and invaluable suggestions. Appreciation also to humorist Tom Antion for advice on humor and grief. To Helane Jeffreys of Voice For Success® for listening skills material and to Deborah Jeffreys Hurley for pre-editing suggestions.

I also want to express my thanks to Phil Gerould, Anne Blish and Karla Nguyen of Crisp Publications for their help and guidance and to Carol Henry for her editing expertise.

DEDICATION—

This book is dedicated to my wife Helane, whose vision initiated this project and who has been both a loving force and inspiration for this work.

INTRODUCTION

Let's face it. No one wants to deal with grief and pain. Many of us run away from people who have had a tragic loss. We want to push loss from our minds because it's just too terrible to hear and think about. It scares us to imagine that the misfortune of others could also happen to us.

We usually associate grief with death and the loss of loved ones. But we all know that grief comes from many sources other than death and dying. The traumatic changes and losses that have been taking place in the workplace for some years now have been like deaths to millions of employees and their families. Their grief is real; it is normal, and there are things you and I can do to help. This book is about how to give that help to others and to ourselves.

By way of introduction, I would like to acquaint you with some basic myths and principles that will help in this process of working with grief.

Common Myths

1. Bad things happen to other people.

2. I can handle this on my own.

3. I don't need to talk about it.

4. No one can tell how really upset I am.

5. My pain, anger and fear will just go away on their own.

6. If I don't think about it, nothing happened or will happen.

Basic Principles

1. You can't fix grief.

2. Everyone grieves differently.

3. There is no set timetable for grief.

4. Grief can come as a result of loss due to change.

5. Grieving the loss of the "old" and reinvesting in the "new" brings about growth and joy.

P A R T

I

Understanding the Origin and Impact of Organizational Change

REALITIES OF WORKPLACE CHANGE

For many employees it is as if they have slipped through a crack in the universe and no longer recognize where or who they are. What was once a secure home-away-from-home has become a frightening, unfriendly and even hostile workplace.

First we will examine some of the realities of transformation in the world of business, and the firestorm of related changes that affect people in the workplace.

Headlines

- 108,946 employees were handed pink slips in January 1994.

- 100,000 U.S. government employees are slated to lose jobs in 1995.

- 600,000 people lost jobs in 1993.

- One-half of Fortune 500 companies listed in 1980 did not make the list in 1990.

- As of 1990, one million middle managers had lost their positions.

- Eight million people lost jobs between 1982 and 1989.

- $171.5 billion in merger deals between January and August 1994, which represents "the biggest merger wave in years."

REALITIES OF WORKPLACE CHANGE (continued)

Statistics = People

Two million jobs cut during the 1980s means two million grieving people and families, and millions more who survive the layoffs but are also thrown into grief by change.

Headlines about the elimination of jobs in well-known companies became noticeable during the eighties. Who can forget the waves of fear that spread from each new announcement during that decade of large-scale cuts by AT&T (27,000), IBM (10,000), General Motors (29,000), Burroughs/Sperry (10,000), and more.

After a change, new management often reduces the total number of departments and staff, reorganizes and relocates the layoff survivors. The results have been fewer middle managers, new reporting relationships and new work groups. The workplace may also undergo physical change. New work may be acquired for a company with a new name. The net effect: a new culture with new expectations, routines, procedures and people. It's not just The New that is the problem. It's leaving The Old culture behind that brings on workplace grief.

CASE: One Impact of Change

I sat in my car waiting for the light to change. A flatbed truck went by, carrying a large commercial sign partially covered by a tarp. The sign said "Roy Rogers™," and I suddenly reacted with anger followed by a low level of sadness. I had heard that Marriott™ was planning to sell the fast-food chain to Hardees™. But when I saw the sign that had been removed from our local Roy's, I felt hurt and a little betrayed at this change in what had been a familiar place and constant visual sign.

Change!

Permanent white water! This is how today's workplace world has been described and will continue to be characterized. A new paradigm has cascaded over what was once taken for granted in the places where we work. We can no longer assume that things will stay as they have been—salaries, benefits, people, locations, company names, job descriptions and job security are all vulnerable to swift and drastic change. The new "psychological contract" between employer and employee does not provide workers with assured continuity in a company. In fact, many business organizations are moving toward work teams and are cutting back on middle managers. Businesses are no longer willing to automatically guarantee employees job security in return for loyalty and work well done. Workers are more and more often considered part-time resources. Increasingly, organizations are judging job continuation on the basis of performance and short-term needs, rather than by family-like emotional ties.

THE HEARTBREAK OF MERGER AND REORGANIZATION

Reorganizing a company or merging two or more corporate cultures represents a difficult transition and provides a challenge for those involved. "The way we used to do the job . . . *the way we were*" is no longer part of the way we are now. People in charge may lose their status. People who have worked in close proximity, who have bonded and served as emotional support for one another, may be separated. A sense of control over the work life can be lost as new leadership takes over.

Watching people terminated with no opportunity to say goodbye leaves those remaining with a sense of dread and a lack of trust in the new management. Social and business networks may be disrupted and the result may be confusion, grief, lowered motivation, anger, apathy and anxiety as well as physical symptoms of depression—aches and pains, physical and mental slowdown, fatigue, illness. The connection between these conditions and lowered productivity is well established.

Before we move on and look at some employee stories that demonstrate the effects of workplace change, take a few minutes to complete the following two "discovery" exercises. They are designed to help you discover some information that you already have stored in your mind. We can quote statistics and headlines to make our points, but the best evidence comes from your own experience. We will first look at your recollections of various changes in the workplace, and then at your observations of employees' grief reactions to these changes.

TAKE A FEW MINUTES TO WORK THROUGH THE FOLLOWING CHECKLISTS

Workplace Change-Loss Checklist

Check the workplace changes experienced by you or someone you know well.
Check M if it was your experience, or O if it was some other person's.

My experience = M   **Other person = O**

	M	O
Hostile takeover	☐	☐
Chapter 11/Bankruptcy	☐	☐
Layoffs	☐	☐
Reorganization	☐	☐
Going out of business	☐	☐
Merger	☐	☐
Downsizing	☐	☐
Redeployment/transfers	☐	☐
Change in technology system	☐	☐
Relocation of company	☐	☐
Restructuring/flattening	☐	☐
Serious drop in business	☐	☐
Loss of CEO/other executive	☐	☐
Outsourcing/use of external service	☐	☐
Serious budget cuts	☐	☐
Other _____	☐	☐
Other _____	☐	☐
Other _____	☐	☐

THE HEARTBREAK OF MERGER AND REORGANIZATION (continued)

Each workplace change event carries with it a multitude of possible reactions. As you recall each of the above experiences, try also to remember any of the resulting reactions you or others had. This exercise of linking workplace changes to employee reactions is the beginning of understanding the process of:

CHANGE = LOSS = GRIEF

Workplace Grief Reaction Observation Checklist

What grief reactions to workplace change-loss have you observed? How does change affect you and your co-workers? Please check any of the items below that you have experienced or observed as a result of workplace change. Check 1, 2, or 3 to indicate the level of reaction that occurred.

1 = Very little　　　　**2 = Moderate amount**　　　　**3 = Significant amount**

	1	2	3
Physical aches and pains	☐	☐	☐
Shouting, raised voices	☐	☐	☐
Absenteeism	☐	☐	☐
Work errors	☐	☐	☐
Apathy	☐	☐	☐
Filing of grievances	☐	☐	☐
Hoarding of supplies and resources	☐	☐	☐
Slow motion	☐	☐	☐
Panic attacks	☐	☐	☐
Fatigue	☐	☐	☐
Hostile conflicts	☐	☐	☐
Anxiety, worry	☐	☐	☐

	1	2	3
Theft	☐	☐	☐
Tardiness	☐	☐	☐
Violent behavior	☐	☐	☐
Pessimism	☐	☐	☐
Anger, irritability	☐	☐	☐
Self-blame	☐	☐	☐
Sabotage	☐	☐	☐
Hurt, crying	☐	☐	☐
Hyperactivity	☐	☐	☐
Isolation	☐	☐	☐
Distrust, suspicion	☐	☐	☐
Feelings of victimization	☐	☐	☐
Numbness	☐	☐	☐
Combat mentality	☐	☐	☐
Denial, avoidance	☐	☐	☐
Self-doubt	☐	☐	☐

What is your estimate of workplace productivity during workplace change?

Productivity =   ☐ Much lower   ☐ Same

Comments: _____

_____

THE HEARTBREAK OF MERGER AND REORGANIZATION (continued)

Cases in Point

Now with these facts in mind, let's go on to some cases of workplace change.

> ### CASE: The Survivor
>
> "They're gone! I looked around the large, open office at the empty work-stations and felt my heart sinking again. At first I tried to ignore those yearning, missing feelings, the hurt for the others and the awful way that the whole place looks so different. And . . . why do I feel so guilty? I even have waves of fear coming up into my body. I never got a chance to say goodbye to some of the people who have been here for years! It was so sudden; they were told to talk to no one, clear their desks and leave."

This employee is grieving the loss of people with whom she had bonded closely, in a way similar to her bond with family members. Now they are gone!

> ### CASE: Where Do I Belong?
>
> "I don't know who I am when I come in here now. Things are so different since the reorganization. I didn't think it would be so bad, but I find myself crying a few minutes after I get here."

The changes in this woman's office—relocation of workstations, staff members sent to other offices, several new managers taking on responsibilities formerly held by longtime supervisors, and a new company name—have created an internal disruption in her perception of the relationship between her work environment and herself. In other words, she does not see herself fitting into this new organizational arrangement.

We expect and enjoy the safety of predictability, of a pattern of continuity in our lives. The terms "solid as rock," "as firm as the ground," "terra firma," have been literally shaken to the core for people who have experienced major earthquakes! In a similar way, the foundation has been knocked from under millions of employees who have experienced the earthquake of organizational change.

> ## CASE: *Fear of the Unknown*
>
> "Now that I've been laid off, it's really a relief! For 18 months we have been waiting for the other shoe to drop! Not knowing if I would be out of a job, and the fear that it *would* happen, kept my emotions on edge. The build-up of tension was a horror."

This man, who has been out of work for six months, talks about the pain of his long-term experience of fearing the worst. He had many physical complaints prior to being terminated, and now he is fighting hard to keep from becoming chronically depressed. This is similar to the feelings of people who are waiting for the results of a biopsy. Both situations could mean a death or death-like loss.

So many employees live with this constant anxiety, once the rumors start flying about mergers, reorganization, downsizing, and other changes. The grieving process begins with *threat* of loss—the first rumors that crackle around the workplace, and the ever-present, haunting "what-ifs."

Please list the changes checked on the **Workplace Change-Loss Checklist** that you have experienced personally.

1. _____

2. _____

3. _____

4. _____

5. _____

As you complete the readings and exercises of this book, you can refer back to these workplace changes as a reference to your own grief reactions.

CORPORATE EVOLUTION AND WORKPLACE CHANGE

The following model and its six principles form the basis for this book.

A Model for Understanding and Coping with Workplace Change, Loss and Grief

1 Volcanic Eruption	2 Workplace Change	3 Employee Loss	4 Grief Reaction	5 Grief Process	6 Healing/ Growth
Markets/ Technology	Reorganization/ Mergers/ Downsizing/ Bankruptcy	Colleagues/ Surroundings/ Security/Trust	Feelings/ Attitudes/ Behaviors	4 Tasks of Healing	Personal growth/ company growth

Let's examine the six principles of this model.

1. Volcanic Eruption

Transformations in the goals and operations are largely due to technological advances and changes in global and national markets.

The impact of changing markets on shareholders' meetings and corporate boardrooms and the urgency of economic survival send shock waves to the very core of workplace grassroots (Drucker, 1992). Add to this the swift technological advances that eliminate jobs and move information throughout the system at lightning speed, and you have the makings of a volcanic eruption in the corporate world. The old ways of organizing to get the job done simply no longer work.

2. Workplace Change

Change manifested as successive waves of downsizing, mergers, restructuring/ reorganization, redeployment and bankruptcy, is now an ongoing part of the business picture.

There is a dramatic shift from a traditional hierarchical management structure to a "cluster" or work-team organization. Managers become coaches rather than bosses (Mills, 1991). Job descriptions are changed or expanded and require new skills. Staff and other resources are scarce, but the same output is still expected. More decisions are made at the work-team level and fewer by managers. Offices are relocated, co-workers left behind, and old familiar routines and cherished equipment and instruments are lost to the workplace change. Fear and uncertainty about the future is the name of the game.

3. Employee Loss

Loss in the workplace is a product of change in the workplace, and this affects employees at all levels.

Perhaps the most overlooked consequences of the turbulent changes in the corporate world since the 1980s are the human factors of loss and grief. How does change in the workplace become loss in the workplace? Whatever we left behind after we have gone through the transition represents loss. Even if The New is desired, we still lose The Old, and the reaction to this loss is *grief.*

When a company alters its organization by reducing or redeploying its workforce, or makes other substantial changes in the way it meets its goals, a sense of loss of *what used to be* is generated for employees. They grieve the loss of people with whom they have bonded, status in the organization, a sense of control over their work, familiar procedures and workspace, trusted reporting relationships, certainty about their future, and their own assumptions about what could be expected from the company (ASTD, 1990). Survivors of layoffs and reorganizations react with feelings like those of people who are grieving a death or the diagnosis of life-threatening illness.

Whenever there is change, there is loss, and loss always brings about some degree of grief reaction. Workplace grief is not given much validity in our society or in its business organizations. As a result, very little space or time is allowed for grieving employees to be off balance, sad, angry, scared, unmotivated, unproductive—in essence, no time is allowed to mourn The Old.

CORPORATE EVOLUTION AND WORKPLACE CHANGE (continued)

4. Grief Reaction

Changes and loss in the workplace result in grief in the workplace. This generates feelings, attitudes and behaviors that are normal and expected reactions to grief.

When companies change to "lean and mean," people become sad, angry and frightened about the future. Their attitudes and behaviors reflect this; work output usually suffers for some interval of time. Managers and Human Resources staff report increased time off, medical complaints and a generally apathetic mood. More errors, a drop in efficiency, decreased creative problem-solving, sabotage and violence have been reported. A *Wall Street Journal* article stated that companies ignoring employees' stress "pay in absenteeism, efficiency and morale problems" (Wall Street Journal, August 10, 1994).

5. Grief Process

There are predictable phases of healing. Workplace grief is no different from any other grief in this sense.

In order to reduce the degree of human suffering and the time of expected lowered productivity, organizations must know what to anticipate in grief reactions, allow sufficient time for grieving, and actively support employees through the healing tasks of grief.

6. Healing/Growth

Healing through grief in the workplace results in benefits to the individual employee as well as to the organization.

The end results for employees who are supported through the phases of the grief process are healing and growth. New work, new skills and new group identity reward individuals with personal growth and development. Organizations are then favored with a healthy transformation of human resources and increased potential for meeting goals.

To review your own firsthand experience with workplace change, complete the following exercise.

EXERCISE: *Your Workplace Change History*

Choose the three most important workplace changes that you have experienced. Write down what was upsetting about each change, and also what was positive about the change.

Change 1: _____

What was upsetting? _____

What was positive? _____

Change 2: _____

What was upsetting? _____

What was positive? _____

Change 3: _____

What was upsetting? _____

What was positive? _____

After doing this exercise, ask yourself what factors or events would have made it easier for you to deal with each change. Jot these down in the space provided below. After completing this book, return to this exercise and add any additional material you have learned.

1. _____

2. _____

3. _____

The workplace change, loss and grief model presented here sets forth the work to be done in the remainder of this book. It provides the basis for understanding the causes and effects of workplace grief.

P A R T

II

What You Need to Know About Grief

WHY ALL LOSS IS DEATH-LIKE

Death comes in many forms. We know that people are expected to behave in a certain way when a loved one has died or has been given six months to live. We also expect grief when a pet has died or possessions have been lost in a house fire. People tell us that they "cried and cried" when they found out that their father has been diagnosed with Alzheimer's and is "no longer the Dad I have always known." Death, however, is not restricted to the end of someone's life. It is currently expanded to mean the ending of something as we have "always known it to be." We are talking about the loss that comes from change.

EXERCISE: Many Faces of Loss

Look at the diagram below. Write into the balloons any of the losses that you have experienced. Add any additional losses in the spaces provided below.

Add additional losses here:

1. _____

2. _____

3. _____

WHY ALL LOSS IS DEATH-LIKE (continued)

Loss has many faces: illness, aging, separation from people and places, unrealized dreams, dashed hopes for the future. When a person we care for dies, a very painful change has taken place. When we move away from a home and neighborhood in which we have lived for several years, we may also feel pain over this death-like loss of friends, familiar shopping and entertainment spots. Loss is the factor that determines our grief. Loss—whether from a death or a death-like change in our life circumstances—hurts.

Learning about how to help with grief is best done when you are aware of your own loss experience. The Change-Loss History exercise will further help you to identify your own past grief reactions.

EXERCISE: Your Change-Loss History

In the spaces provided, write down three losses you can remember from your past, from childhood on. These can be a death, loss of a pet, loss of a work or other role, or any loss due to an important change in your life. Also, circle the number that best indicates how much each loss remains a part of your thoughts and feelings.

**Not much
current thought
or feelings**
                                                                        **Constant
current thought
or feelings**

Loss 1: _____

0	1	2	3	4	5	6	7	8	9	10

Loss 2: _____

0	1	2	3	4	5	6	7	8	9	10

Loss 3: _____

0	1	2	3	4	5	6	7	8	9	10

After you have completed the above, take a moment to recall the circumstances surrounding the loss with the *highest* rating.

What was helpful for you at the time of loss?

_____

_____

_____

What was not helpful for you at this time?

_____

_____

If you were a child, what did you hear from adults about loss and the expression of grief?

_____

_____

_____

Compare your reactions to more recent loss with the way you handled loss in the past. Make a note on any differences you have identified.

_____

_____

_____

_____

Now that you have inventoried some of your own past personal losses, let's find out why loss hurts so much.

ATTACHMENT BONDING AND LOSS

I struggled against the ocean current, which was pulling me into the jutting rocks of the breaker. I worked hard to resist the urge to just give in and not try anymore. My son tried a rescue from a rubber raft, but I waved him away— fearing he would be crushed against the rocks. My heart was pounding! I felt utterly exhausted and my resolve to survive was fading. I heard myself saying, "Is this it? The end?" Somehow I managed to grasp the edge of a rock and held on for dear life—long enough to gain the strength to pull myself up onto the top of the breaker ledge and to safety.

The instinct for survival, to *hang on for dear life,* is a basic human drive. Animals babies literally cling to the fur of the mother, and people hang on to their self-image, to each other, to routines, dreams and favorite things and titles, *for dear life.* These are examples of the attachment theory developed by Dr. John Bowlby, who studied the way babies and small children acted when they were separated from their mothers (Bowlby, 1980). We attach early to a mother or mother substitute in order to survive, and the attachment behaviors—staying close, hanging on, reaching for the person or other object of attachment—continues throughout life. Attachment behavior leads to the creation of bonds. *The way we make and break bonds in the early part of our lives determines how we will deal with connecting and letting go in later life.*

Sigmund Freud said that we not only mourn the loss of people, but we grieve for the loss of such intangibles as self-image, dreams and health (Freud, 1917). Not only do we grieve for broken bonds—tangible and intangible—but we also begin to grieve as soon as there is a hint that a bond is threatened. That basic infantile attachment-for-survival is the energy source underlying each bond that is formed. That is why we may panic when health, a relationship, office organization or job description is threatened with ending or with significant change: It can feel as threatening to our survival as an infant's separation from its mother.

To help you explore your own attachments in the workplace, complete the following Workplace Attachment Survey.

Workplace Attachment Survey

List the five most important aspects of your current job. What would you miss the most if you were transferred or if the job were significantly changed?

Current job title: _____

What features of my job would I hate to lose most?

1. _____

_____

2. _____

_____

3. _____

_____

4. _____

_____

5. _____

_____

You may be surprised after doing this exercise at some of the things you want to keep. Now ask yourself why each one is so important, and what else may be lost *in addition to* the item or feature of the job?

THREE CONDITIONS OF GRIEF

People grieve in three kinds of situations:

1. We grieve when we *lose something:* a loved one, a pet, a job, our wallet, a workplace friend, a familiar role in an organization, the old "family" atmosphere at work, our identity in the workplace. This represents breaking the bond or significantly altering it, and the grief reaction begins.

2. We grieve when we are *threatened with the loss* of something or the possibility of significantly altering a bond: going in for a biopsy or other medical tests, a child very late and still not home from school, rumors of layoffs, top-level management meetings with known competitors.

CASE: A Perceived Loss

In a company whose financial situation was known to be shaky because of the loss of several large contracts to competitors, a middle-level manager was having severe stress-related complaints—insomnia, loss of appetite, difficulty in concentrating and a sense of dread each morning. He was able to pinpoint the onset of these symptoms to the first time he became aware that his boss was not acting his old, friendly self. This vice president's shift from warm, familiar conversation to more formal, abrupt communication signaled the alteration of their bond, and a slow panic began for the middle manager. This led to many "what-ifs," "supposes," and the sick feeling in his stomach that was the beginning of the grief reaction process.

---

3. We also grieve for something that we *never had and never will have.* This represents our perceived failure to bond. Examples are the relationship never to be had with an alcoholic mother or a brother who died in a war, an education never acquired, the career never attained, the dream of a lifestyle never achieved. A company's financial reverses and the resultant changes often contribute directly to the loss of dreams for not only the employees but also for the families affected. What we don't get to have because of workplace change and uncertainty creates multiple grief reactions.

CASE: *Facing Many Losses*

Tom and Sue were planning a second child, and were house-hunting in order to have more room for their growing family. Tom had been a foreman at his plant for seven years. He was known as a hard worker and loyal team-player. Tom had taken courses in the local community college in business and management and was aware that he was being considered for promotion to assistant manager. When his company was bought out by an aggressive competitor, Tom was notified by his manager that the division was to be reorganized and that new work teams would replace the current subgroups. Team leaders were being sent in from the new company headquarters, and Tom would have to take a team member role or there would be no place for him in the new organization. He would no longer be reporting to his old boss and would share a desk out in the production area. There would be no change in benefits, but his salary would be reduced.

Tom is now faced with the loss of his immediate career development plans, threat of loss of the desired new home, as well as the actual loss of his role and title of foreman, loss of his reporting relationship with a friendly and supportive boss, a change from his own little office to sharing a desk, and the uncertainty of the new work teams. He is, in fact, faced with a multiple-loss situation. There are many Toms who, for one reason or another—family needs, poor job market, fear of making a change—never get the education, the promotion or the lifestyle they hoped for. These missing pieces of life provide a continuous source of grief for employees and for their families. Keep in mind that whatever change-loss grief employees are experiencing, the loved ones affected by this loss are also grieving. This grief bounces back and forth between the family and the workplace and can intensify until either some help is given or something breaks down.

THREE CONDITIONS OF GRIEF (continued)

Recall Exercise

1. List the three conditions under which a person will grieve.

    a. _____

    b. _____

    c. _____

2. What is the fundamental purpose of attachment and bonding? _____

    _____

    _____

3. In addition to people, what can we bond to? _____

    _____

    _____

We encounter many forms of loss as we move through life. Our earliest bonding is for survival, and this energy exists in all bonding. We attach to people, places and things, and when the attachment bonds are broken or threatened, we experience pain and other feelings of loss. How we make and break bonds in early life provides the basis for how we react to and heal from grief as adults.

HOW EMPLOYEES FEEL DURING AND AFTER WORKPLACE CHANGE →

The Feelings of Grief at a Glance

Sadness:	Pain of loss, emptiness, hurt feeling. "Like a motherless child."
Anger:	"I *had* something—a job description, a title, working relationships, familiar routines and procedures—and they've been taken away from me!" "I'm mad!"
Loss of trust:	"It's NOT FAIR! I did a good job for all these years, I was a loyal employee, and now look what they've done to me! I feel betrayed!"
Fear:	"Am I next? What is going to happen to me? To my family? Will I survive the next reduction sweep?"
Confusion:	"Who am I now? How do I fit in? What am I to the organization?"
Physical aches and pains:	"Ow! My back, my neck, my head, my stomach!"
What's-the-use attitude:	"Why bother? This work can wait. Who cares!?"
Yearning, regret:	"I wish things were back *the way they were.* I feel like a step-child in a new family." "I miss the good old days."
Return of old grief:	"This reminds me of when we lost . . ."
Guilt:	"It's my fault. If I were better at my job or smarter . . ." or "I should have seen the handwriting on the wall."
Shame:	"I feel so stupid. No one in my family has ever been demoted or transferred out."
Helplessness:	"I have control of *nothing* at work anymore!" "I'm just a lame duck."
Marital and family distress:	"My unhappiness at work has spilled over into my home life." "We argue a lot at home now."

UNDERSTANDING EMPLOYEES' FEELINGS

How willing are we to hear how someone else feels? "How are you?" "How's it going?" and "What's up today?" are frequently used as greetings. But are we really receptive to hearing that someone is angry, hurting or scared? Not only are we reluctant to hear about how another employee feels, we usually don't want to share all that much about how we ourselves feel. Feelings . . . We can't deny that they exist, yet our society generally wants that kind of communication kept private, very private.

The "OK" and "Not OK" signals about expressing anger, fear and sadness are part of our early development. Statements such as "Don't raise your voice!" "Cry baby!" "Keep crying and I'll really give you something to cry about!" "Don't be a baby, there's nothing to be afraid of"—early childhood messages about specific feelings or feelings in general—set the example for the level to which we do or do not express feelings in later life. When we get the message that feelings are "Not OK," we tend to hold in or suppress our feelings. When a life change-loss event occurs and the normal reaction is to express appropriate anger, sadness or fear, *we stuff it.*

Feelings are further blocked by business organizations that view the expression of negative feelings or even confusion about workplace change as *having a bad attitude.* The results of this repression are, typically, physical symptoms, depression, anxiety, lowered morale and lessened motivation, stress reactions and burnout.

Let's take an in-depth look at the typical feelings that are part of the normal grieving process.

Anger

Take a rattle from a baby and there is no mistaking the cry of anger. Take computer privileges away from a teenager or deny use of the family car, and be prepared for rage. Take a title, desk, parking place, job security, workplace friend or feeling of trust away from an employee, and anger is a natural reaction.

We express anger whenever we are denied something we want, or perceive obstacles to our goal placed in our way. Have you ever gone over to the copier with a rush job, only to discover the machine is out of order? Or found yourself stuck in traffic with an appointment just minutes away? Frustration converts to anger very quickly and is a natural, normal release of an inner emotional state. How many of us really enjoy having to pack up our office and move our things to a new location? Some employees say, "It's enough to make you scream!"

Anger is an expected reaction to loss and one of the natural emotions of human beings. A baby is not bad or wrong because it cries with anger when a toy is taken away. An adolescent is not wrong or bad when he or she expresses anger as a result of adversity or loss. An employee is not a bad person because he or she gets angry when something or someone has been taken away. In every one of these examples, the *normal* reaction includes anger. The trouble starts when we either ignore the anger or engage in unhealthy expressions of the anger.

Unresolved anger can lead to chronic bitterness, self-hatred, grudges and an ongoing sense of helplessness. In some cases, it can also lead to physical aches and pains, symptoms of stress, depression and other emotional disorders. However, anger that is *constructively* managed can fuel productive change and bring about motivation to develop new skills and complete important tasks.

EXERCISE: *Identify Your Anger*

List five things that make you angry both at work and away from work.

1. _____

2. _____

3. _____

4. _____

5. _____

ME? UPSET?

UNDERSTANDING EMPLOYEES' FEELINGS (continued)

 Pain

"It hurts, it hurts so much!" The young widow was sobbing in my office, recalling the few happy years she had with her husband who had died several weeks before in an accident. Her pain of grief—that aching feeling inside, the "emptiness" that grievers describe—is well known. A week later, another woman was engaging in very similar grieving behavior. She had been laid off from a job she loved, and described the same aching, empty feeling inside. When our bonds (with people, places, routines and even things) are broken, the physical and emotional pain of grief occurs along with anger as a part of the process. For people who have made their work and the workplace social environment the most important part of their lives, the loss or threat of loss of The Old can result in devastating pain.

As we grow and develop from infancy to adulthood, we learn who we are from important people around us—parents, brothers and sisters, other relatives, teachers, friends, colleagues and bosses. Part of our identity is tied up with our workplace role and how people around us act toward us. We read our OK-ness in the eyes of those important others, and when we are separated from them because of workplace change, the source of personal validation is lost . . . and grieved. The importance of workplace friends and associates takes on greater meaning in our mobile society where, for many, co-workers are *extended* family.

EXERCISE: What Causes You Pain?

1. In what way do you see the pain of workplace change as being like the pain of a death?

   _____

   _____

   _____

2. What kind of emotional pain in another person is the most difficult for you to see?

   _____

   _____

   _____

Fear

"I'm scared, Mommy—how will we get money to live now? "How will I survive this?" "What will happen to us?" "Who will take care of us?" These are the words of people who have just lost a loved one or learned of a life-threatening medical diagnosis. Because the bottom-line issue in loss is survival, the threat or actual breaking of a bond causes fear and sometimes panic and terror. Children, especially, are very blunt about their fears regarding economic security. When one parent dies, children express great concern for the health and well-being of the surviving parent.

Loss due to workplace change often causes employees to express similar fears about security and worries about the future. Loved ones, especially children, will express anxiety about how the family will live should the employee be laid off or moved to a lower-paying job with no hopes for career advancement.

Fears may be specific, such as fear of the loss of a home, of children's opportunity for education, loss of health benefits or material possessions. Fears may be more general, such as having to face the family or friends or neighbors, or the overall future, if the job is lost or income is reduced. Older workers may fear that they cannot learn the skills required in The New.

Old childhood messages about not expressing fear may keep worries unexpressed and underground, and therefore become a source of stress and physical and emotional problems. Many will find themselves distracted by these fears, and work performance will suffer as a result.

EXERCISE: *Uncover Your Fears*

1. What is your biggest fear about your job at this time?

_____

_____

_____

2. How does this get in the way of your job performance?

_____

_____

_____

UNDERSTANDING EMPLOYEES' FEELINGS (continued)

Guilt

"It's my fault." "I feel like I've been punished for being bad." "What did I do wrong!?" "I just wasn't good enough." "I wasn't a good enough spouse, lover, parent, son or daughter, sibling, friend, manager, co-worker, employee." It is not uncommon for a lot of soul-searching to occur after a loved one has died or is bedridden with a terminal illness. Bereaved people will frequently think about the many regrets they have, and what they should or shouldn't have done.

Similarly, employees who are about to be transferred, undergo a significant job-role change, or who are in that limbo between company layoffs may find many regrets surfacing regarding their work history. Facts often do not support any connection between an employee's performance and the redeployment or other change in status. Nevertheless, many who survive a layoff—only to have their work situation profoundly altered—see this as a result of something lacking in their own performance or personality.

EXERCISE: Getting Through Guilt

1. When you or someone you care about feels guilty, what seems to help the most?

_____

_____

_____

Shame

"I can't look my co-workers in the eye anymore." "Since I lost my supervisory role, I'm too embarrassed to even eat in the cafeteria." "I just know the whole neighborhood is talking about what's going on." "I can't face my parents now that I have been demoted." "I don't even tell people I meet where I work now."

The part of us that is our work identity may get lost when reorganizations, mergers and redeployments occur. We're not on the same team anymore, or not part of the decision-making process, or have lost some of the trappings of workplace status. We are ashamed and reluctant to let friends and neighbors know what is happening.

Shame is an expected reaction to loss and to change that results in lowered status. It is related to the guilt feelings discussed above, in that it comes from not feeling OK about our identity now that significant changes have taken place. Shame and guilt have their roots in early childhood messages we receive and record about what is good and right, and about what gets us love and acceptance.

EXERCISE: Is Shame OK?

1. If someone asked you if it was OK to feel ashamed, what would you say and why?

   _____

   _____

   _____

GRIEF REACTIONS TO CHANGE-LOSS

In the following Grief Reactions to Change-Loss chart, you will have an opportunity to see the connections between grief-reaction feelings, attitudes and behaviors. We have listed some of the many feelings, attitudes and behaviors that are grief reactions to loss in the workplace. Take a few minutes to look over these three categories of reactions. Think about any workplace change-loss that you or someone you know has experienced. Then circle any items that you or the other person have experienced.

FEELINGS	ATTITUDES	BEHAVIORS
Anger	"Oh, yeah!?" Resentment, bitterness "The hell with it!" "I'll get even." Gallows humor	Hostile acts Lowered productivity Destructiveness Stealing Work left undone Errors Sarcastic joking
Pain	"What's the use!" "Nothing matters. Why bother?"	Withdrawal Isolation Low efficiency Low energy Errors
Fear	"Don't stick your neck out." "Play it safe." Apathy	Rigidity Uncreative, boredom Tentative action Errors "Holding on" to staff, resources
Guilt	Self-consciousness "I've been bad." Negative self-concept "Excuse me for living." "I should have been the one let go."	Hiding Nervous Errors
Shame	"I'm not good enough." "They don't like me." "I want to run away."	Hiding Avoidance Isolation Errors

UNDERSTANDING ATTITUDES AND BEHAVIORS

DISTRUST: After the shockwave of a sudden reorganization announcement and the layoffs and other changes that typically follow, employees may feel as though "the rug has been pulled out from under them." The trust level with the company takes a nose dive, and people who feel betrayed develop a generally suspicious, "save-your-own-skin" attitude. Some organizations have reported suspicion among peers and a withholding of information for fear of advancing somebody else's interests.

RESENTMENT: Bitter resentment, especially toward those "above" in the organizational hierarchy, can develop as the known and secure workplace becomes cold and uncertain. For many, there is a need to blame someone and a desire to "get even." This can result in work slowdown, lack of teamwork or follow-up, and even hostile, destructive behaviors.

APATHY: "What's the use of working hard?" When employees see hard-working, dedicated co-workers get laid off, it undermines their own motivation to produce. Not knowing what the future holds puts work effort in limbo for many, and apathy produces absenteeism, overlong breaks and inefficiency.

DESPERATION: Nervousness, hyperactivity, undue anxiety to please the boss are how some employees respond to changes and the threat of more change. "If I get more paperwork out, start the day earlier and stay later, come in on weekends, maybe I'll get to stay or keep my staff or this office." Stress and its negative effects usually accompany this behavior.

PLAY IT SAFE: When you live with the axe ready to fall, there are fears that taking risks and setting work goals too high or being too creative may result in displeasing the boss. Goals are set low, creative approaches to problem solving are scarce, and no one wants to take any chances of looking bad. Everyone holds their breath; while things are on hold, so is productivity.

HELPLESSNESS: "I'll never be able to get the job done." "There is no support and I have to do it all by myself." "I'm afraid to ask my supervisor for help." For many, there is a sinking feeling of low self-confidence, and this contributes to apathy or bitterness and even hostile, destructive behavior.

When employees are showing the above attitudes and behaviors, the chances of a high level of productivity are poor. Let's find out why.

GRIEF REACTIONS AFFECT PRODUCTIVITY

Take another look at the chart of Grief Reactions to Change-Loss in the Workplace and some of the reasons for lowered productivity will be obvious.

NO LOYALTY: Grieving people, who are hurt and bitter and have no sense of security, experience a significant drop in loyalty to company goals.

REVENGE: Many say they will seek revenge in any way possible. Others simply go through the motions to get through another day and put out little real effort. For still others, anger influences the work pace and causes missed deadlines, lost contracts, theft and sabotaged projects.

ACCIDENTS AND ERRORS: Some people become so frantic that they are prone to accidents and errors that might not normally occur.

LOW MORALE: The lowered morale of employees who feel unfairly treated or are embittered by friends' layoffs drains energy from the work force. The worry about what may still be lost is a powerful distraction. This is similar to trying to get your job done while you are worried about a loved one who is critically ill. People feel that there is a cloud hanging constantly over everything, and this is carried into their home lives as well.

AVOIDING WORK: Coming to work is not pleasant; tardiness, absenteeism, and medical complaints increase. Drug and alcohol abuse may also occur or increase as employees fall back on self-medicating to deal with the constant workplace agitation and related home conflicts.

HOLDING BACK: Managers may set easily attainable goals to minimize risk of failure.

STRESS: The threat of loss and the grief over what has already been lost increases stress levels. The ongoing stress of unattended grief has psychological as well as physical repercussions. The net effect of this consumption of energy is the lowering of productivity in both hidden and obvious ways.

EXERCISE

List any additional reasons you may be aware of for lowered productivity during workplace change.

_____

_____

Review

The feelings of hurt, anger and fear, and the attitudes and behaviors of grief reaction, are normal and expected human responses to loss. When grief is unattended, the stress, energy drain and negative attitudes have a direct effect on employee productivity. Inefficiency, errors, slowdown, medical complaints and generally low morale all contribute to lowered work output, more time off and, in some cases, even theft and sabotage.

III

The Process of Grief

WHAT IS GRIEF?

Grief: A Definition

Grief is a set of reactions to loss or the threat of loss. Grief includes feelings, attitudes and behaviors that exist over a period of time. Among affected people, the nature of the reactions vary, as well as the length of time they persist.

Different Tears for Different Folks

It's true! Look around and you will notice that people grieve differently. *There is absolutely no one "right way" to grieve a loss.* You have doubtless observed that some people cry pretty openly at a time of sorrow; others appear free of emotion. In the workplace, some employees will want to "talk about it"; others will keep their feelings to themselves. Some tears are on the outside, and some tears are on the inside.

A person may go in and out of grief reaction, experiencing waves of sadness, anger and fear. Some individuals will need many weeks or months to work through grief and reach a place of healing and resolution. Others seem to stay in grief forever. Still others who have experienced loss show no grief reactions at all, and deny any internal grief feelings.

It is normal to grieve when you have experienced a loss. How much and how long is influenced by three factors:

> 1. **PERSONALITY AND PAST LOSS HISTORY**
>
> 2. **NATURE OF THE CURRENT LOSS**
>
> 3. **SUPPORT DURING THE GRIEF PROCESS**

WHAT IS GRIEF? (continued)

1. Personality and Past Loss History

▶ The way bonds have been made and broken in the past will influence how a current loss is grieved. A history of successful letting-go of bonds and attachments will give the person the confidence and skills needed to go through the new grief process and move to healing. Old, unresolved loss will complicate the grieving process. An employee may be overwhelmed with feelings from an old loss when a new loss has occurred.

▶ The learned personal style of dealing with life issues as the employee matured will influence how much and how long the person grieves. Some people are more expressive about their feelings, and grieving will flow along. Others are more prone to run away from feelings, and this is what they will usually do with grief.

▶ Current physical or psychological distress will affect the employee's ability to grieve and heal. When an employee is already depressed or suffering from a physical ailment, grief may be aggravated.

2. Nature of the Current Loss

▶ How many actual losses are involved? A transfer may mean more than losing surroundings and people. Routines, status, networks of resources, even the friendly cook in the cafeteria and easy parking may also be left behind. Every loss is a multiple loss.

▶ What is at risk? Change in the workplace may place career advancement at risk. It can open up questions about "Who am I in this reorganized workplace?" "Am I still a valuable employee?"

▶ Will I ever be safe and secure here again? When employees feel there will never be an end to the insecurity, the grief process is prolonged. Knowing there is a light at the end of the tunnel provides a safe destination at the end of the grief.

3. Support During the Grief Process

► How much help is given by the organization, both before the change takes place and during the actual grieving process? Lack of information, advance notice, time to grieve or support activities during the grief process will send an unsympathetic message of noncaring. This typically aggravates the grief reactions and prolongs the interval of time before healing. (See Preparing for the Effects of Workplace change on page 74.)

► How much support is made available by friends and family? Outside help from family, friends and clergy will provide the employee a source of strength and stability during the grief process. Lack of understanding and conflicts at home will increase the employee's vulnerability and difficulty with the grief process.

THE POSITIVE EFFECT OF ANTICIPATORY GRIEF

Once the initial announcement of proposed change has been made, employees begin the grieving process. Grief starts early on, as imaginations create worst-case scenarios. This is as true for the threat of workplace change-loss as it is when we are waiting for the results of a fearful medical diagnosis. For employees taken by a surprise announcement, the effect is similar to a sudden death and the trauma of the loss may be intensified because of the shock.

When employees can have some preparation for the coming change, anticipation of The New and letting go of The Old can actually be visualized. The feelings of grief start with this internal imagery. Grieving in advance of coming loss due to workplace change is what psychologists call anticipatory grief.

This start-up of mourning behavior is useful in that it provides a mental rehearsal for what is yet to happen. The "head start" on grieving can reduce the amount of time it takes to complete the grief work after workplace change has occurred. When a loved one is terminally ill, the grief begins with the diagnosis, or even earlier when the person is having tests for suspicious symptoms. When the loved one dies, there is still the pain of loss and other grief reactions, but much of the grief may have already taken place.

Thus, the more advanced notice of workplace change, the greater opportunity employees will have to engage in anticipatory grief.

BOWLBY'S BASIC PHASES OF LOSS AND MOURNING

John Bowlby, M.D., of the Tavistock Institute of Human Relations in London studied the reactions of very young children to separation from their mothers. He developed an outline of what happens as a result of this separation (Bowlby, 1980). Because we believe that all attachment and bonding has a basic survival function, this has a direct application to the reactions of adults dealing with significant loss. It is as if there still is a "little one" inside each of us, who reacts as a child would to loss or the threat of loss. It is important to note that people may move back and forth in these phases and may overlap phases.

► **PHASE I:**

Protest of the loss, and attempts to recover what was lost. A time of yearning for the lost object or situation, despite no hope for recovery of what was lost. A time of anxiety and wishful thinking about that which was lost.

► **PHASE II:**

Despair sets in as hope fades for recovery of what was lost. A period of longing, apathy, hostility and sadness. A breaking down of the old bonds; disorganization; pulling away and mourning. This phase is critical to the growth and healing of the next phase.

► **PHASE III:**

Reorganization takes place after detaching from what was lost. The grief work has been significantly addressed, and new attachments have been or are being made. Without the breaking of the attachments in Phase II, reorganization is incomplete at best and usually impossible.

BOWLBY'S BASIC PHASES OF LOSS AND MOURNING (continued)

To help expand your understanding of how people grieve, please do the following exercise.

EXERCISE: Bowlby Phases of Grief

Think of someone you know fairly well outside of the workplace—a family member, friend or acquaintance—who has had a loss to deal with. Describe what the person did or what they said with respect to each of the Bowlby Phases of Grief.

Briefly describe the loss situation: _____

_____

_____

Protest Phase: _____

_____

_____

Disorganization/Despair Phase: _____

_____

_____

Detachment/Reorganization Phase: _____

_____

_____

Implications for the Workforce

Bowlby's phases make it clear that a complex set of reactions occur after a separation or loss. Employee attempts at recovering what has been lost may take the form of holding on to work equipment, resisting a move to a new office location, lunching only with former colleagues, filing grievances and other actions to stop change, and other forms of written and vocal protest.

When employees are actively feeling and expressing grief emotions—anger, hurt, fear—they have entered Bowlby's Disorganization Phase. This is a time of decreased work effort and increased emotional and physical complaints, as well as the attitudes and behaviors described on pages 34–35.

The period of grief and despair for employees who survive an organizational transition is a necessary and valuable phase of grief. The grief work enables them to let go of The Old and begin to attach to The New. This is the critical period for organizational help; *it is important to provide time for grieving and support programs.*

During the Reorganization Phase, employees begin to look ahead to a new picture of "Who am I?" at the other end of the transition. This is the next part of their healing-through-grief journey, and it requires a new identity. It is a time for an inventory of skills, the development of new skills and even the setting of new work and career objectives.

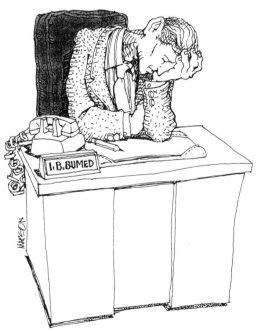

KÜBLER-ROSS STAGES OF LOSS

Let's take a look at the stages of loss identified by Elisabeth Kübler-Ross, M.D.

KÜBLER-ROSS STAGES OF LOSS

Denial	"No! Not me!"
Anger	"Why me?" "Not fair!"
Bargaining	"Not yet!" "What can I do?"
Depression	"Go away!" "I'm too tired"
Acceptance	"OK." "If that's the only way."

It should be noted that the boundaries between the Kübler-Ross stages are fluid, and people may find themselves in more than one stage at the same time. One can move back and forth from denial to acceptance and back again. A person who is working on acceptance might move over to depression or anger or denial, and back to acceptance again. A dying man says he feels ready to die. He has handled all the necessary arrangements, said goodbye to loved ones, and feels a sense of contentment about the completion of his life. He appears to be very much in the acceptance stage. Then one day he grows quiet and then suddenly looks up and says, "No! No! This can't be happening to me." He is able to revisit *denial* for a while and then returns to *acceptance*.

These stages were identified by Dr. Kübler-Ross as a result of her observations of dying patients, and they have come to be used to describe anyone dealing with loss (Kübler-Ross, 1968).

Stage I—Denial

"Oh no!" "I don't want to hear it!" This phase is characterized by changing the subject when conversations about change come up; pushing away thoughts about the painful reality; continuing to use old forms, procedures and labels. The "old guard" sticks together at lunchtime, keeping a distance from the "new people."

These are examples of *denial*. Denial has an important function when a loss is about to happen or has already occurred. For many, diverting the reality of the loss makes it possible for them to gather needed inner adjustment skills. News of a death or frightening medical diagnosis is usually met with some form of denial. People actually hold their hands up with palms outward and physically *push* the bad news away. Loss or the threat of loss is painful to think about, and no one wants pain. Someone answers the phone, and you know they have received bad news when they cry out "NO!" We simply do not want to let it in.

Denial allows the upsetting news to slowly seep inward. Too often we hear people criticized for being "in denial." Some period of denial is natural, however, and expected during the early stages of grieving a loss. There is no exact timetable for when denial should end. It will vary for each type of change-loss and for each person. As discussed earlier, our own history of making and breaking bonds will shape the way we deal with loss in the present.

Imagine a cartoon showing an executive holding a gun and a knife. He orders his secretary to bring him some files and says that if she acts as if he has not been laid off, no one will get hurt.

We don't want to let go of what has been so much a part of who we are. To let go of this piece of our identity is allowing a part of ourselves to die. This is painful and we want to delay, push it away, pretend it isn't happening. We hope for a last-minute rescue, a change of heart by the board of directors, a miraculous new contract. *This is denial, and it is a normal reaction to loss.*

KÜBLER-ROSS STAGES OF LOSS (continued)

Stage II—Anger

"Why me?!" "It's not fair!" "Why now, after all these years?!" "How could they do this to (me)(him)(her)?!" "I hate them for this!" Rage, resentment, bitterness, sabotage and violence can result from the *anger* phase of loss and grief. When you have something or someone and you lose what you had, a primitive anger is the result. Anger, too, is an expected part of the grieving process. People are not bad or wrong for feeling angry. What *can* be bad or wrong is what is done with the anger.

Anger due to loss or threat of loss can be displaced to someone or something other than the source of the anger. When a loved one dies or receives a life-threatening diagnosis, the anger may be directed toward a Higher Being, a medical staff, the government or anyone else. Loss in the workplace can bring about the dumping of anger on the old management, the new management, co-workers, family or even the family pet.

Anger may be expressed directly, as a hostile attitude, words or behavior. Grumbling, excessive questioning, complaining, angry facial expressions, arguing, fighting, insubordination, destruction of property, theft, acts of physical violence and in some instances homicide have all been reported in the workplace experiencing change.

Anger can also be expressed in a passive or indirect way. Lateness, absenteeism, work slowdown, increased errors, decreased cooperation, lack of follow-up efforts, and diminished self-direction are examples of passive aggression.

Stage III—Bargaining

"Maybe if I come in earlier and stay later I'll survive the next layoff." "Can we keep these procedures for a little while longer?" "Is there any way that I can keep my office? My desk? My parking space?" "I'll even work for less money if I can stay in my old division."

When faced with loss, people usually try to keep the bonds to The Old as intact as they can. In the face of life-threatening illness, a person may bargain with his or her Creator and promise to pray regularly, eat healthier, quit smoking or drinking, exercise, act "nicer" and generally improve his or her lifestyle. Loved ones may secretly promise to be kinder than ever to the ill person, to pray, to give to charity and do whatever they can to *hold on to what was*.

In the same way, workplace loss causes similar negotiating in order to *hold on* to The Old.

Stage IV—Depression

"I feel like someone has died." "It's painful to come to work now." "I hurt inside and don't even want to come here anymore." "I find myself crying and wanting to run away." "I think of any excuse not to come to work." "What's the use?!"

Workplace change brings about a real sense of death. The actual loss of people, work routines, location, or control disrupts an important part of the person's total identity and meaning in life. The sense of knowing what to expect from the organization and what is expected by the organization is also lost, as new psychological contracts are forged in a shrinking work environment.

These losses are felt with varying degrees of pain, and result in a period of mourning and in some cases withdrawal. Isolating behaviors are not uncommon. Eating lunch or taking breaks alone, sad facial expressions, sighing, and other body language that signals "Leave me alone!" are part of the depression of grief. The energy level of the depressed individual decreases and may directly affect work output, error control, teamwork, effective communication, tardiness and absenteeism.

Stage V—Acceptance

"Now that I have been given a lemon, I'll have to make lemonade!" "Now that I have had a chance to get some of these feelings out, I can start to write that new job description." "Well, if you can't beat them, join them!" "I'm still not happy about this change, but I'm going to look at this as a challenge rather than a punishment."

Acceptance is primarily an intellectual state. It means that the person has accepted the inevitable. Being emotionally OK with the change may not necessarily be part of the early period of this phase. A dying person may get his or her financial affairs in order, complete unfinished business with loved ones and develop a strong spiritual sense, yet still not be all that happy about the coming profound change.

An employee who is about to be uprooted from a familiar workplace setting and given a new job and title may reconcile the changes in an intellectual way by tying up loose ends, saying goodbye to work friends and looking at The New as a *professional challenge.* However, the employee may retain many negative feelings about the change and will take some time to achieve an emotional adjustment by creating new bonds to people, place, routines and organizational identity.

It is this rebonding that brings about a total acceptance to The New and a completion of the grieving/healing process. At this time there is a balance between the head's and heart's acceptance of workplace change.

KÜBLER-ROSS STAGES OF LOSS (continued)

In the next exercise you will be able to use a personal workplace change-loss situation and apply the Kübler-Ross stages to your experience.

EXERCISE: Stages of Loss

Choose the **most critical** workplace change-loss situation you have experienced. List your recollections about your own behaviors, with respect to each of the five Kübler-Ross stages of loss.

First, briefly describe the loss situation: _____

_____

_____

- *Denial:* _____

_____

_____

- *Anger:* _____

_____

_____

- *Bargaining:* _____

_____

_____

- *Depression:* _____

_____

_____

- *Acceptance:* _____

_____

_____

HOW THE OLD PAIN GOT THERE AND WHERE IT GOES

From *childhood* messages that we receive from parents or other important grownups, we learn if it's OK to say how we feel, or even if it's OK to feel emotions at all. So many of us as children perceive that it is *not OK* or *not safe* to express how we feel. We grow up with this message and, as a result, in situations such as workplace change-loss, we push anger, hurt and fear down; we *stuff it.*

For example, anger should never be destructive to self or others. However, if you were told, "You have no reason or no right to be angry!" or "Get out of here or I'll really give you something to be angry about!", then you may be in the habit of pushing anger down. Any childhood message that tells the child that it is not OK to have feelings or to even let anyone know that you have feelings will cause accumulated unresolved anger, sadness or fear. Whenever a loss occurs and the normal thing to do is to feel and express emotion, the person who has learned that it is not OK will again stuff the feelings.

HOW THE OLD PAIN GOT THERE AND WHERE IT GOES (continued)

To help you to more fully understand the influence of childhood messages on current grief, complete the following exercise:

EXERCISE: Childhood Messages

Directions: This exercise focuses on three important grief feelings—anger, sadness and fear. Imagine yourself back in your childhood. See how much you can recall of your early childhood messages from parents or other adults about feelings. Was it OK to be angry, to cry or to be afraid?

1. Under the Childhood Messages column, briefly state what you recall hearing as a child about each of the feelings—**Anger, Sadness/Crying** and **Fear.**

2. Then rate how much you *still behave* according to the old messages.

FEELINGS	CHILDHOOD MESSAGES	CURRENT RATING
		(How much message is still in effect?)
		10 = Very Much Very Little = 1

10 9 8 7 6 5 4 3 2 1

Anger: _____

_____

10 9 8 7 6 5 4 3 2 1

Sadness/crying: _____

_____

10 9 8 7 6 5 4 3 2 1

Fear: _____

_____

Completing the Childhood Messages Exercise will help you gauge how aware you are of the current effect of the old messages. Not all of the messages you received can be recalled, but they still may influence you, whether you know it or not. Unfinished business around old losses for which you were not allowed to grieve will be stored in that internal pot of stuff that has been filling up over the years.

The Unfinished Business Model

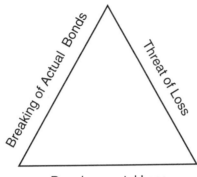

Developmental Loss

1. Developmental Loss

First, we store up loss material from the natural and expected changes that occur throughout our normal development: starting school, getting a new brother or sister, leaving home, our first job . . . Each time there is a change or transition that is a normal part of life, there is the loss of what was. If we never are given the opportunity to express any feelings about these changes, the feelings are stored.

2. Breaking of Actual Bonds

Second, we store up loss material when bonds we have made are broken. People we love die or move away, pets die, a beloved toy is lost, our family moves to a new city, friends reject us, we are dropped from a team or lose a job. As described earlier, whenever an attachment bond is broken, there is grief, and grief wants to cry, rage and so forth. If we have been denied the right to express these feelings, we store them.

3. Threat of Loss

Third, we store up loss material when we live under constant threat of loss, such as chronic financial insecurity, an abusive family life, very low self-esteem, a parent or sibling who is gravely ill, an unsafe environment. Because this threat of loss of someone or something is ongoing, if not managed, it creates highly destructive and painful unfinished business and is stored.

THE COST OF STORING OLD PAIN

► *Wasted energy.* We pay a price in energy consumed each time we stuff a feeling into that storage bin filled with old grief, anger, fear, shame and guilt. The energy used to keep the lid on this bin of old baggage is thus unavailable for other, more positive purposes in our lives—solving problems, loving, being creative, accomplishing our work. The more we store, the more energy is needed to hold down the accumulated stuff.

► *Accumulated unfinished business* filters into every aspect of our behavior. Doctors and nurses bring their unfinished business to the bedside of every patient. Corporate managers carry their unfinished business into each decision they make. Employees faced with current grief due to workplace change-loss also carry the echoes of old unfinished grief. The old stored feelings mingle with the new grief and, worse, often we are not aware that this is happening. When the pool of stored negativity is too full, even a small crisis can result in an overreaction. The lid blows off the storage bin and causes a more severe grief reaction.

► *Chronic stress reaction* is another cost to the individual of keeping the old loss material under control. This increases the risk for physical and emotional symptoms, as well as for burnout and an inability to work through the grieving/healing process (Jeffreys, 1990).

Review

As we move through life, unfinished loss material is stored within us. The extent to which we learned to express feelings vs. stuff feelings determines how much material is stored. Storing unfinished business takes its toll on a person physically and emotionally. When a new loss or crisis occurs, the old, stored material mingles in and becomes part of the grief reaction. We are not always aware that this is happening.

P A R T

IV

Helping Employees
Cope with Workplace
Change-Loss Grief

UNDERSTANDING THE TASKS OF MOURNING

Earlier we discovered that anger, hurt, fear, confusion, guilt and shame are typical parts of the grief reaction. We have also studied the sequence of phases and stages experienced by a person dealing with the various reactions to loss or threatened loss. The grief reaction is a psychological trauma just as a wound or a burn is a physical trauma. The grief reaction process is an attempt to reestablish the individual's emotional balance in the same way that physical healing reestablishes the body's well-being. Thus, in order for individuals to recover their equilibrium, *grieving behavior is necessary.*

To complete the grief process, the person must address each of the Four Tasks of Mourning, as described by Harvard Psychologist Dr. J. William Worden. Failure to work on each of these Tasks will result in incomplete mourning, and the person will store unfinished loss pain (Worden, 1991).

> **Task I:**   Accepting the Reality of the Loss
>
> **Task II:**   Reaching the Pain and other Feelings of Grief
>
> **Task III:** Make the Needed Changes for a New Work Situation
>
> **Task IV:**   Develop a New Group Identity and Make New Bonds

Task I: Accepting the Reality of the Loss

For an employee to let go of The Old, its loss must be acknowledged. An individual must face the fact of the ending of what was and that things will never be the same again. People may attempt to avoid and deny that a change has or is about to occur. They may resist any acknowledgment of the "endings." They may resist any acknowledgment of new personnel who represent "new beginnings."

A parallel example is a young child who knows a new baby is coming into the family. The child may not want to think about it, may have bad dreams about it or even try to "make it not come." Once the new baby is home, the child must face the reality that the family organization is forever altered and the child's place in the family—as the only child—is gone forever. The child may cry, act helpless, and demand attention as though still the only child, and may resist the reality of the end of "what was." Many employees "don't think about it"—and when the change really occurs they are taken by surprise.

UNDERSTANDING THE TASKS OF MOURNING (continued)

Denying the reality of the loss can also take the form of ignoring the significance of the loss. "No problem!" "I wasn't so crazy about that old job anyway!" "Those people in my other office weren't so wonderful after all." People can go in and out of believing and denying that the change has taken place or is about to take place.

A man sits, his head in his hands, sobbing in pain. He has been redeployed to another office in his division. His pain is over being separated from work friends who had become a support for him over the years. When he sits up and wipes his face, he says it is "probably a good thing" that he is being transferred. That it would be better for his career. He mentions several other benefits to the change—and then the tears begin to well up in his eyes again. His intellect or "head" has accepted the reality, but his emotional self or "heart" has not. We call this the "Head/Heart Split." People often find it easier to let go of The Old with the head but continue to hold on with the heart.

How to Help with Task I

1. **Talk about what is being lost** as a result of the change. An employee who is unable to acknowledge openly that the change has or is about to happen needs help to do so. Encourage him or her to say out loud what he or she is losing as a result of the workplace change. In this way the reality of the situation will be more likely to come to the surface.

2. **Talk positively with the employee about the value of The Old** and honoring its contributions to the individual as well as to the company. This helps to place The Old in the past.

3. **Use a "goodbye ritual."** This can be very helpful, especially when employees are changing locations. It can be done informally, by looking at the area and saying goodbye to whatever was special about the space, or by writing the goodbyes down on paper. Take photos and put them up in the new place.

4. **Create a "memory book" or "memory letter"** and share it at a group meeting.

5. **Bring some familiar objects—wall hangings, desk accessories, a piece of carpet—from the old setting** to the new location, and place them in symbolic spots there.

6. **Take employees to visit the new staff** and new location. If possible, have them visit The New before officially beginning.

Task II: Reaching the Pain and Other Feelings of Grief

The pain of grief is physical as well as emotional. Often, a person who has experienced loss will say, "I feel as though I have been punched in the stomach." Any type of loss can bring about those hurting, aching, empty feelings. It is important that people allow themselves to feel these feelings and to tell someone about them as well. It is also important that people assisting those who are grieving be accepting of that pain and that it must be experienced in order to avoid *getting stuck in grief.*

Others' pain can be hard to take. It's not easy to stay with them when they start to worry, cry or rage about changes in their work role. Each individual will experience the pain and feelings of grief differently. If you are in a position to help another employee because of your job role or because you are a friend or colleague, you may or may not be comfortable with the expression of these feelings. Changing the subject or inventing distractions for such people may be unproductive for their grieving/healing process. Some see tears as a sign of weakness, or anger as lack of control, or worrying as a lack of courage. But we can be most helpful when we view the sounds of grief as sounds of healing.

Completing this Task requires feelings and expressing the feelings of grief. (See "Helping People Heal By Listening" on page 66.)

How to Help with Task II

1. **Listen! Listen! Listen!** Spend time—go for a walk, have lunch; let them know their feelings are normal. Postpone your own agenda in favor of theirs.

2. **Offer specific help** with some of their work, if possible. Refrain from giving advice or sharing your own past misfortunes. *After* some of their feelings have been expressed, knowing someone else has gone through a similar workplace change can be of help.

3. **Refrain from distracting** them when they are "in feelings."

4. **Encourage them to keep a journal** of feelings and thoughts about the change-loss.

5. **Avoid setting deadlines** for "getting over this."

6. **Help them seek professional help** if things get out of control. (See "Helping an Employee in a Grief Reaction" on page 71.)

UNDERSTANDING THE TASKS OF MOURNING (continued)

Task III: Make the Needed Changes for a New Work Situation

The work of this Task is to adjust to the new workplace environment. This requires facing the work day in a new space or with new people, without the old social network, and with the use of new or rusty skills. The person may be growing aware of just how important the "old gang" was in making the work day pleasant and quick. The reliable colleague who was always available to answer questions is not so handy anymore. The location of supplies, operation of office and work equipment, routines and schedules may be different and strange. Commuting and parking arrangements, lunch facilities and even dress code may involve additional areas of adjustment.

Perhaps the most significant issue for many will be "How do I fit in here?" The individual's previous group identity and the formation of a new one is already on the minds of workers even during the earliest announcement of a change. A Human Resources staff member of a major transportation company stated that people began asking this question at the very beginning of a major restructuring. This concern over what will be the individual's niche in the new organizational structure was reported to be a dominant concern.

There may be resentment at having to develop new skills, prove oneself again, figure out where things are kept, learn how to use new equipment, make new friends. There may be irritation at not having the same level of support services as in the former workplace setting. People may find themselves feeling less in control, helpless, inadequate. Old childhood issues of "not good enough" or "not lovable" may be triggered.

Adjusting to the reality of constant change is of particular importance. The loss of continuity in one's work life as a result of the *permanent white water* phenomenon creates an ongoing need to adjust and readjust. However, this need for flexibility creates a "When is it going to stop, already!?" atmosphere.

Grief following relocation is attributed to loss of continuity of familiar surroundings and the existing social bonds (Fried, 1963). The new psychological contract between corporation and employees implies an ongoing need to adjust to disruption of continuity. "Just when I thought everything was settled, we've got another new change to deal with!"

When people do not adequately address Task III, they may resist learning new skills and remain in a state of helplessness, requiring much assistance and supervision. Or they may stay isolated from the work group whenever possible. Much of the resistance to adjusting to the new work environment is a result of the employee not accepting that the change is permanent. The work of Task III is a critical turning point for completing the grieving/healing process. *Failure to adequately address this task will result in unresolved grief and the storage of unfinished loss material.* Such a condition will usually leave both the employee and management very unhappy.

How to Help with Task III

1. **Get information** about The New work situation as soon as possible.

2. **Identify the new skills and learnings** needed to get the job done.

3. **Locate training for new skills** (in-service training and program external to the workplace).

4. **Help with new location arrangements** (equipment, desks, storage space).

5. **Help the employee see the move or change as part of a total career picture.**

Task IV: Develop a New Group Identity and Make New Bonds

A newly transferred employee may continue to maintain ties with work friends in the former organization. The bonds are typically not severed in one quick cut. The detachment from people, surroundings and routines of The Old takes time, but eventually the individual will look to The New as *home.* Visits to the former group and phone calls to former colleagues begin to diminish. Workplace needs are, more and more, filled by the new colleagues; less time is spent thinking about what was.

The energy from old bonds is now being invested in new bonds. There is a new reaction by the employee to memories of The Old, and fewer feelings of grief are generated. The person begins to reorganize his or her own view of the new workplace situation, with the former work group recognized for its past value.

UNDERSTANDING THE TASKS OF MOURNING (continued)

The employee finds a place in the workplace world for the thoughts of what was, and this interferes less and less in the new work tasks. "I know who I am in this new work situation and how I fit in." To fail in Task IV is to insist that "I can't let go of The Old and will not bond with The New." Personal traits, unfinished loss material, poor transition management and lack of organization in The New can all contribute to an employee's inability to accomplish Task IV.

How to Help with Task IV

1. **Provide orientation** to the new work situation.

2. **Create informal social contacts** with others in the new situation.

3. **Organize team-building activities** with the new work group.

4. **Assist employees with meeting their personal needs** in the new situation.

5. **Provide opportunities to talk about The Old** and "how we did things then."

6. **Acknowledge the value of former** experiences and relationships.

7. **Create new rituals and traditions** for The New, such as welcoming ceremonies and other forms of personal recognition.

EXERCISE: Four Tasks of Grieving/Healing

Choose one workplace change you have experienced. For each of the Four Tasks, indicate how much still needs to be done to reach a degree of completion, by circling the responses that best describe your current feelings.

Briefly describe the workplace change:

_____

_____

_____

_____

Task I: Accepting the Reality of the Loss

(a) "Still have a lot to do." "Can't believe it happened yet."
(b) "Going in and out of believing it happened."
(c) "Pretty much believe now."
(d) Other _____

Task II: Reaching the Pain and Other Feelings of Grief

(a) "A lot of painful feelings have come up about this change."
(b) "Some painful feelings came up about this change."
(c) "Very few feelings came up about this change."
(d) Other _____

Task III: Make the Needed Changes for a New Work Situation

(a) "I've done what I need to do—learned new skills, adjusted to new routines, created new work schedules for the new situation."
(b) "I'm still working on getting the new skills and understanding the new routines."
(c) "I haven't yet been able to adjust to the new work situation."
(d) Other _____

Task IV: Develop a New Group Identity and Make New Bonds

(a) "I really feel like I fit in with the new group."
(b) "Most of the time I feel like I fit in with the new group."
(c) "I'm still working on fitting in with these new folks."
(d) Other _____

Based on your responses above, what do you think you need to do to more adequately address any of the Tasks rated (b) or (c)? Review the "How To Help . . ." material after each of the Four Tasks in this section.

_____

_____

_____

The Four Tasks of the grieving/healing process set forth the work that must be done to complete grieving and reach a state of healing and growth. There are specific ways to facilitate accomplishing each Task. You can use this material to help yourself or to help others.

HELPING PEOPLE HEAL BY LISTENING

Much of the help we give to others in accomplishing these Tasks requires that we truly be available to hear what they say. To be an active listener:

- Avoid premature advice-giving or trying to fix grief.

- Keep your attention focused on what the other person is saying, deferring to his or her agenda.

- Avoid asking questions that begin with "Why. . ."

Remember: YOU CAN'T FIX GRIEF! But you *can listen* to a person who is grieving. A listener who is comfortable because he or she knows that the expression of feelings is a normal, healthy response to grief can be of tremendous help.

When listening is done in a passive, disinterested way, the listener appears to be wondering "When will this be over?" Such a listener usually fails to make eye contact, is easily distracted by any other activity in the area, and frequently changes the subject from the grief issue. The grieving person will quickly become aware of the lack of interest and will usually terminate the conversation and avoid the person in the future.

Helpful listening, on the other hand, is done in an active way. This lets the grieving person really feel heard. The active listening approach is an important skill for helping people who are dealing with loss or threat of loss.

Five Steps to Helpful Listening

The five steps to helpful listening do not have to take place in sequence. They can flow together or can occur in combination and build on each other.

STEP 1) Show interest nonverbally.

Face the speaker, make eye contact, nod and use expressions and body language to indicate *I hear you.* Be careful not to indicate judgment by such facial and body expressions as the raised eyebrow, shoulder shrug or turning away from the speaker.

STEP 2 Show interest verbally.

Use affirmative sounds or words such as "Uh huh," "Mm hm," and "I hear you." Step 2 is a continuation of Step 1 and also requires a nonjudgmental and receptive attitude. Avoid comments that block the flow of expression from the grieving person, such as "I hate to hear that!" "Don't tell me that." "Oh, no!" However, it is acceptable if you feel sorrow to let tears come. This is a time to say, "I'm sad, too."

STEP 3 Open the conversational door.

So far, you have been active in attending to the speaker through nonverbal behavior and by making brief sounds or phrases that affirm your attention to the speaker. You can now increase the level of participation by using statements that clearly encourage the grieving person. Statements such as "Yes, go on," "Tell me more," and "I'd like to hear more about that" will directly invite the grieving person to talk more about a particular issue.

STEP 4 Rephrase the speaker's content. (Listen for meaning!)

In this step, say back to the speaker, in your own words, the essential meaning of what you heard. This is called *paraphrasing* and it has three advantages:

- It lets the grieving person know that he or she really has your attention.

- It provides an accuracy check on what you believe was said.

- It tells the speaker he or she has been understood from an intellectual standpoint.

Here are a couple of examples of paraphrasing: "So you have given up making any career plans since the downsizing started." "It sounds like you don't even want to come to work anymore." Being accurately understood keeps grieving employees from feeling isolated and enables them to continue dealing with their own painful reactions.

This is not the time for you to give advice or talk about your own worries. It is still the speaker's agenda and this must be respected.

HELPING PEOPLE HEAL BY LISTENING (continued)

STEP 5   Say what the listener feels. (Listen for feeling!)

This is a feeling-level response and assures the grieving person that he or she is being understood at the emotional level. The helping listener will determine how the grieving person feels by what has been said and by what has been communicated through facial expression and body language. The speaker's tone of voice; slowness or rapidity of speech; sad, angry or frightened face; tears; words of anger or cursing; hand and arm gestures, slouching of body, and shaking of the head—all this *as well as* the content of what is being said provide clues as to how the speaker is feeling. You are seeking the *emotional music behind the words.*

The goal in this step is simply to tell the speaker what you believe he or she is feeling. For example, "You're really *angry* about how you were told about the transfer." "You seem *frightened* about what is going to happen to your job." "I can see how *upset* this change is making you." "You're *worried* about how you will fit into the new organization." Using words such as *upset* or *angry* or *hurt* will let the grieving person know that you truly know how he or she feels. Being understood in this way allows grieving people to release pain and other emotional energy, helping them to move along the road of the grieving process toward healing.

Practice the five active listening skills on friends and family, and notice the different way they begin to respond to you. Work on the first three steps for a week or two, and then start to use the paraphrasing and feeling-response techniques of steps 4 and 5. People in general appreciate begin heard and understood. Individuals dealing with the distress of grief reaction are especially in great need of this kind of helpful listening.

Now try the Helpful Listening Exercise, and check your answers with the recommended responses that follow.

EXERCISE: *Helpful Listening*

Following are three statements you might hear from a person dealing with transition grief. For each statement, write a response that communicates to the grieving person that *you know the feelings they are having.* For example:

Grieving person: "I don't know what I'll do if they cut my hours."
Helping listener: "You're pretty worried about that."

Grieving person: "I hate the way they 'retired' Mary and Jack."
Helpful listener: "That made you pretty angry."

1. **Grieving Employee:** "I hate the way they just don't tell you anything."

   Your helpful listening response: _____

   _____

2. **Grieving Employee:** "It's so gloomy and empty in here now that the transfers have been made."

   Your helpful listening response: _____

   _____

3. **Grieving Employee:** "Now that we have been reorganized, I don't know what will happen to my career."

   Your helpful listening response: _____

   _____

Suggested Helpful Listening Responses

There is no one perfect way to respond to a grieving person, but these suggestions can be used for each of the above employee statements.

1. "It really gets you angry to be kept in the dark." or "You really get mad when you don't know what's happening." or "It's upsetting not to know."

2. "You really seem sad about the people who are gone." or "This place really depresses you now."

3. "Sounds like you're scared about your future." or "That's a big worry for you, isn't it?"

HELPING AN EMPLOYEE IN A GRIEF REACTION

Here are some general suggestions for helping someone else through workplace change-loss grief.

- Accept their feelings without judgment.

- Handle your own upset feelings.

- Deal with the grieving person's anger.

- Use humor when it is appropriate.

- Know when to get more specialized help.

General Suggestions

▶ **If your own loss material comes up** while helping someone who is grieving, put it aside for the moment and talk to a friend about it later. And be sure you *do* talk to someone; it's very difficult to help anyone when your own unfinished business keeps surfacing.

▶ **Don't be afraid of silence**—it can be golden for a person in pain. Just stay with them.

▶ **Let the speaker know it's OK to express feelings,** to cry, to say what is in their hearts.

▶ **Honor confidentiality.** Be very careful not to repeat to others what has been shared with you.

▶ **Keep your commitments.** If you say "Let's have lunch and talk," be sure you follow up.

▶ **Allow enough time to be with the grieving person.** Don't start a conversation when you have another commitment in a few minutes.

▶ **Use humor.** Humor can be a healthy outlet for a grieving employee, allowing him or her to temporarily step outside of grief and decide what needs to be done about the situation. Some research shows that laughing releases brain chemicals that aid in problem solving. However, the use of humor does not necessarily mean that employees who joke about workplace change-loss are "handling things well." They will still need assistance and support.

It is important to use your helpful listening skills at all times. Though it may be tempting to respond with your own humorous comments, first *listen* to the employee, and then acknowledge the humor with a smile and nod. Laughter can be good medicine. It can soften the pain of grief reaction. Avoid jumping into a "trade-you-jokes" routine, which may interfere with the grieving person's agenda. Sometimes the expression of humor about their upsetting work situation is a prelude to tears or anger.

Humor can also be a way of expressing anger and resentment. Sarcastic joking and cynical comments may in reality be expressions of deep pain and anger that the employee hopes will be disguised. Use your effective listening skills in this situation.

► **Be alert to signs of trouble:** These signs might include extreme changes in behavior, talk of suicide, idle threats of homicide, lack of appetite or insomnia, use of drugs or alcohol, extreme withdrawal, extreme social activity, unusual irritability, many physical complaints. Such employees should be referred to Employee Assistance, Human Resources, the company nurse, clergy, or a mental health professional.

What to Avoid

► **Don't ask too many questions.** Questions can stop an employee's expression of feelings.

► **Avoid platitudes** such as, "Everything will work out" or "This is the Creator's will." Employees who are hurting may not be able to accept this. What they need most at first is to be heard—without judgment.

► **Don't try to minimize feelings.** Never say "You really shouldn't feel that way" or "Now, now, it's really not that bad " or "You're lucky you still have a job."

► **Don't take anger directed at you personally.** Grief-reaction anger frequently spills out onto people who do not deserve it. This will diminish as the person vents his or her feelings. Remember, you are not the object of their anger. Use the five helpful listening skills, and repeat back to them that you see how angry and upset they are. This acknowledgment usually helps the angry person hear his or her own rage.

QUICK TIPS FOR HELPING

1. **LISTEN.** No advice.

2. **STAY CONNECTED.** Make contact; don't avoid.

3. **TALK ABOUT WHATEVER IS BROUGHT UP.** Follow *their* agenda.

4. **ASK ABOUT FEELINGS.** "What concerns you most about the reorganization?"

5. **AVOID TRADING "WAR STORIES" AT FIRST.** After the employee has had a chance to do some grieving, hearing about your change-loss experience may offer some hope.

6. **REMAIN NONJUDGMENTAL IN THE FACE OF STRONG EMOTION.** Keep in mind the feelings are *theirs*.

7. **HELP START THE CHANGE PROCESS ANY SMALL WAY.** Help with moving things, putting new names in a Rolodex™, obtaining new organizational charts, reviewing or creating new performance objectives.

8. **HELP THEM KEEP PART OF THE OLD SYSTEM AS THEY ENTER THE NEW ONE.** Save some visual symbol, such as an old logo, photos.

9. **HELP BREAK THE ICE WITH NEW STAFF.** Arrange for the employee to have lunch with one new team member.

10. **SHARE INFORMATION ABOUT THE NEW SYSTEM.** Tell anything hopeful you know about the new management.

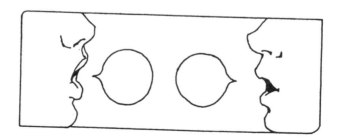

EXERCISE: *Helping a Co-worker Through Grief*

Think of a person who is currently dealing with workplace grief. If you were to help them now, which of the above tips for helping would you plan to use?

List these skills for assisting the employee.

1. _____

   _____

2. _____

   _____

3. _____

   _____

4. _____

   _____

5. _____

   _____

Remember:

- You can't *fix* grief, but you can *listen* and offer specific *help.*

- It's the grieving employee's agenda, not yours.

- Your own stuff may come up while helping someone else. See this as an opportunity for your own personal growth.

- Use your helpful listening skills at all times.

- When behaviors or emotional conditions worry you, suggest that the employee see someone who has specialized skills for further help.

As individuals, we can offer our attention and assistance to grieving colleagues who are experiencing grief due to workplace change-loss. We may do this because we are a friend, or because it is a responsibility of our work role.

PREPARING FOR THE EFFECTS OF WORKPLACE CHANGE

Managers, Human Resource specialists, Organizational Development consultants, Employee Assistance staff, industrial health nurses and consulting mental health professionals are all in a position to help employees cope with grief. So are the co-workers of grieving employees. Responsible organizations will provide the necessary training opportunities for staff identified to assist employees through the grief process.

Preparation for dealing with workplace grief must start with an understanding of grief and its predictable phases. Reading and completing the exercises of this book will provide a good basic understanding of normal grief and how to help employees cope and heal.

In addition, people who want to help others with grief must be aware of their own unfinished grief issues. Managers who are fully occupied with the effects of workplace change and uncertainty will need to attend to their own grief reactions, too. Don't make the mistake of believing, incorrectly, that you are exempt from grief reactions and must put on a strong, unemotional face. You may fool the people around you, but you won't fool your own body and mind. By acknowledging your own grief material, old and new, and talking with someone else about it, you will increase your value in the task of helping other employees.

Ten Commandments for Organizations Coping with Workplace Change

I. Provide a continuous flow of accurate and up-to-date information about the coming change, throughout the entire process.

PROBLEM: A lack of accurate, current and official information will power the rumor mills, causing much unnecessary anxiety, pain and low trust. Further, without definitive word from an authorized spokesperson, employees will incorporate their own fantasies and can grieve needlessly.

COMMENT: One senior director of a government agency undergoing reorganization and requiring massive redeployment has set up monthly "Town Meetings" to keep 1,100 employees informed of the latest developments.

Other organizations use memos, e-mail, and unit meetings to keep the valid information flowing and the rumors down. Human Resources professionals have commented that a lack of information creates a climate of uncertainty, which feeds anxiety much the same as waiting for the results of a biopsy.

II. Maintain a personal knowledge base regarding predictable patterns of change-loss grief reactions, and the skills for responding to people who are mourning.

PROBLEM: If you don't know what to expect from a grieving person, the feelings can be very upsetting to you.

COMMENT: Your comfort level in being with a sad and angry employee will be raised if you anticipate certain feelings, attitudes and behaviors. Additionally, having helpful listening and response skills, as well as specific helping techniques, will increase your comfort and reduce your own stress.

III. Maintain awareness of your own personal loss and grief issues that may be activated by the change-loss.

PROBLEM: Managers often struggle with their own loss issues in times of change. Failure to acknowledge this in some way will increase personal stress and decrease availability to help others.

COMMENT: All persons in the midst of a corporate transition, regardless of their roles, are subject to grief reactions. Talk with a close work friend, a consultant or someone outside of the organization. Writing down your feelings and concerns in a private journal can help to relieve some of the grief. Externalizing your grief material will relieve the pressure and increase your effectiveness in helping other employees.

IV. Maintain current awareness of the realities of the specific change-loss and its effects on all employees.

PROBLEM: When managers avoid dealing with the effects of workplace changes on employees, they cannot plan for employee support. Denial of the reality of a change-loss situation can block out information about what is really going on in the hearts of employees.

COMMENT: One director has arranged for over 1,000 employees to have direct access to him via confidential, anonymous e-mail. Each day he can read what people are feeling and concerned about and can respond to the messages personally on a computer bulletin board.

PREPARING FOR THE EFFECTS OF WORKPLACE CHANGE (continued)

V. Acknowledge the value and contributions of The Old.

PROBLEM: When employees feel that their former organizational unit or group has been attacked or its value discounted, they typically react with anger, defensiveness and resentment of The New system.

COMMENT: Rituals and ceremonies, even letters of acknowledgment of the value and contribution of the old group, will facilitate letting go of The Old and moving toward The New.

VI. Provide for continuity between The Old and The New by creating transitional roles, reporting relationships, and organizational groupings, and by generating informal and formal organizational means to keep people feeling that they are still a valued part of the organization.

PROBLEM: During the in-between time, there is an increased possibility of instability, confusion, and anxiety.

COMMENT: Provide temporary titles, appoint transition teams with specific tasks, and provide frequent updated procedures as the transition moves along. This gives employees a feeling of control, of structure and stability. Don't let acting titles become permanent.

VII. Provide opportunities for people to grieve, by providing ending rituals for The Old as well as formal and informal grief support services.

PROBLEM: When no opportunities to express the feelings of grief are provided, those feelings are stuffed or go underground. When feelings are not expressed and there are no regular avenues for channeling fears and other concerns, the employee lacks an internal support system for addressing the Four Tasks of Mourning. The effect of this is "getting stuck in grief."

COMMENT: One executive provided small groups of employees an opportunity to express grief and ask questions at a regularly scheduled roundtable.

An ending ritual, at which an entire department or other group says goodbye to "the way we were," helps with letting go. A formal history of the group/ department/unit can be created by the employees. A memory book of symbolic photos can be assembled and shown at the goodbye ceremony. Planting a tree or putting up a plaque in honor of the old group can also help with looking to the future instead of the past.

Save some decorations, a piece of equipment or some symbolic items from The Old setting to be placed in The New. These can be a photo of the group or company, a logo, or a photo of the old office or building.

Hold meetings for explaining the relationship between change in the workplace and grief in the workplace, and what to expect from grief reactions and the process of grief.

Weekly support groups and individual counseling can also be an important contribution to supporting employees through the grieving/healing process.

VIII. Provide opportunities for people to discover, as soon as possible, the part they will play in The New.

PROBLEM: Not knowing their planned future role poses a major threat to employees facing workplace change. This breeds anxiety. The identity and social network developed in The Old is not transferable to The New. There is uncertainty about who one will be, how one will be accepted and how well one will do in the new group.

COMMENT: As soon as possible, give employees an opportunity to learn what the new system will be like. Orientation to location, equipment, other staff, schedules and procedures will help to give employees a sense of the new work environment.

Where new skills are required for new job descriptions, training should be provided sooner rather than later. Knowing what is expected will reduce employee anxiety and establish clear work goals. For many, these specific objectives may help to reestablish career goals. The loss of dreams and hopes as a result of workplace change is as hurtful as more tangible losses.

PREPARING FOR THE EFFECTS OF WORKPLACE CHANGE (continued)

IX. Recognize that employees will be at best ambivalent and possibly resentful in The New, and will require time to complete the tasks of the grieving/ healing process.

PROBLEM: Impatience with the time it takes employees "to get over it" and "get up to speed" can actually slow down their movement through the grief process.

COMMENT: Everyone grieves differently and has a different grief time-frame. If you can get a sense of where a particular employee is in the Four Tasks of Mourning, it will direct you in how to help them. Review "Understanding the Tasks of Mourning" on page 59 to determine how you or someone else can facilitate the addressing of the appropriate Tasks. Note: Employees who remain in denial for an extremely long period (who never really address Task I) will need special help.

X. Create a ritual celebration for The New, and symbolize the new identity of the group and its individual members.

PROBLEM: When the organization fails to note the passing of an era—the ending of The Old—it becomes more difficult for affected employees to let go.

COMMENT: Resistance to letting go of The Old was reported by one manager, who described employees bluntly refusing to leave their old offices. This was so in spite of the fact that the new offices were in elegant new buildings. In one company, people literally held on to their desks when the relocation coordinator walked through the door.

An organization-wide ritual to "pass the mantle" to The New will help to face the employees toward the future. An example of this is the creation of a new logo or emblem that includes part of the old symbols. Both formal and informal rituals involving the new employee groups will help to establish a new identity for employees. As energy is withdrawn from the old attachments and reinvested in The New, healing takes place.

Review

Following are four tasks that an organization must accomplish in order to provide adequate grief support to employees:

Four Tasks for Organizational Grief Support

1. Give Employees Frequent, Accurate Information

2. Allow Employees Time to Grieve

3. Provide Support Services, Including Rituals, Support Groups and Counseling

4. Offer Training in New Work Skills and Grief Support Skills

---

Suggested Half-Day Employee Grief Support Workshop

Consider holding a four-hour grief support workshop, perhaps led by someone in-house. The workshop should be in a quiet, undisturbed space. Be sure time is provided for participants to express their feelings. During this workshop, it is important that the leader use the helpful listening skills presented earlier in this book. This is an opportunity for employees to learn some facts about workplace grief and what to expect regarding their own grief process. Here is the schedule:

1/2 hour **Introduction to Change-Loss Grief**
Leader presents, using the material in Part II (page 17) of this book.

1 hour **Loss History Exercise**
Individuals complete the exercises presented in "Why All Loss Is Death-like (page 19)."

1/2 hour **Discussion of Individual Responses to Loss History Exercise** (page 20)

3/4 hour **Group Exercise: "Workplace Change Stories"**
Leader starts, then each participant relates his or her workplace change-loss experience. The leader facilitates a discussion of feelings generated by the changes and follows with what support people need with regard to their feelings.

1/2 hour **Application to Workplace, and Homework**
Create a goodbye ritual or other "letting go" activity (page 60) and have a group discussion of what support is available to employees.

WORKPLACE GRIEF: THE ASSETS AND LIABILITIES

*"If you go through the tumbler of life, you
can come out crushed or polished."*

Elisabeth Kübler-Ross, M.D.

As we travel through life and experience its expected and unexpected twists and turns, we may look back at the journey and see that crisis and loss have pushed us in new directions, and that these have been good directions. It is possible to acknowledge "the gift of loss." This does not mean that we wanted the loss to occur or that we would still not want to recover whatever was lost: a person, good job, career dream. Yet the loss has happened, and we grieved the loss and were able to move on to other pathways that eventually led to healing, growth and joy.

So, too, can we consider traumatic workplace changes, loss and grief as a detour in life's roadway, leading us to new skills, new work, a new career and the possibilities for renewed joy and satisfaction in life.

Understanding the natural and expected flow of human reactions as employees move from The Old to The New will enable managers to intervene with clarity and compassion. There is a transition time between The Old and The New that lacks needed anchors and grounding for people undergoing change. Special attention must be given to the grief process during this time. To ignore this grieving process will extend the period of human pain and of lowered productivity.

Review

Grief is a process that begins with an actual loss or threat of loss. The nature of grieving behaviors and the length of the grieving process varies by individual. It is influenced by employee personality, nature of the change-loss, and the degree of support received. Grieving people experience predictable phases and stages of grief behavior. When grief work is completed, they reach a point of acceptance and healing.

A FINAL STATEMENT

Everyone grieves a little differently, and the timetable for mourning varies by individual. Grief isn't right or wrong—it is just a normal human reaction to loss. The loss can be a death or some other very important change in a person's life circumstances. Managers, Human Resources staff, co-workers, and others can help this process along by attending to the human needs for letting go and facilitating new beginnings.

It isn't easy to be close to another's pain and try to offer help. Someone else's loss and grief can easily trigger our own unfinished grief and make it hard to be with them. Acknowledging and airing our own stored grief issues can make it easier. So, too, can knowing what to expect from a grief reaction, as well as acquiring some skills in helping another. Here is where you can make a big difference to an employee who is in grief. The comfort your skills and knowledge will give *you* lets you stay with the grieving person when others cannot.

We typically resist change. Familiar routines, procedures, organizational relationships and workplace culture are hard to let go of. Yet, given the right individual and group support, there can be a light at the end of the tunnel. You can even realize a gift from workplace change-loss: the gift of new possibilities for both the employee and the organization.

The corporate family can create new traditions for a new culture.

With careful handling, someday people will look back at the time of workplace upheaval and sincerely acknowledge the difficulty of the changes. They will also give thanks for the courage of people who had no choice but to make changes in their work, in their lives and in themselves.

BIBLIOGRAPHY AND RECOMMENDED READING LIST

American Society For Training And Development, *Info-Line,* October 1990.

Autry, J. A., *Love and Profit: The Art Of Caring Leadership,* Morrow, NY, 1991.

Bennett, A., *The Death of the Organization Man,* Morrow, NY, 1990.

Bolton, R., *People Skills,* Touchstone, NY, 1979.

Bone, D., *The Business of Listening,* Crisp Publications, Menlo Park, CA, 1994.

Bowlby, J., *Sadness and Depression,* Basic Books, NY, 1980.

Bridges, W., *Managing Transitions,* Addison-Wesley, Reading, MA, 1991.

Buono, A. F., and Bowditch, J. L., *The Human Side of Mergers and Acquisitions,* Jossey-Bass, San Francisco, 1989.

Covey, S. R., *The 7 Habits of Highly Effective People,* Simon & Schuster, NY, 1989.

Drucker, P., *Managing the Future,* Truman-Talley-Tutton, NY, 1992.

Fossum, L., *Understanding Organizational Change,* Crisp Publications, Menlo Park, CA, 1989.

Freud, S., *Mourning and Melonchalia* (1917 Standard Edition of Complete Psychological Works of Sigmund Freud), Vol. 14, Hogarth Press & Institute of Psychological Analysis, London, 1957.

Fried, M., "Grieving For A Lost Home," in Duhl, J., (Ed.), *The Urban Condition,* Basic Books, NY, 1963.

Jeffreys, J. S., *Get It Out: The Externalization of Emotional Pain,* J. S. Jeffreys & Associates, Columbia, MD, 1990.

Kübler-Ross, E., *On Death and Dying,* Macmillan, NY, 1969.

Mills, D. Q., *Rebirth of the Corporation,* Wiley, NY, 1991.

Noer, D., *Healing the Wounds,* Jossey-Bass, San Francisco, 1993.

Pritchett, P., *After The Merger: Managing the Shockwaves,* Dow Jones-Irwin, 1985.

Schlossberg, N., *Overwhelmed: Coping With Life's Ups & Downs*, Lexington Books, Lexington, MA, 1989.

Scott, C. D., and Jaffe, D.T., *Managing Change at Work*, Crisp Publications, Menlo Park, CA, 1989, 1994.

Wall Street Journal, "Marketplace," August 10, 1994.

Woodward, H., and Buchholz, S., *Aftershock: Helping People Through Corporate Change*, Wiley, N.Y., 1987.

Worden, J. W., *Grief Counseling and Grief Therapy*, Springer, NY, 1991.

Feedback Form

In order for us to improve our concepts, cases and exercises, we welcome and encourage feedback from our readers.

Please tell us:

What about this book was especially useful? _____

_____

_____

_____

What suggestions for improvements do you have? _____

_____

_____

_____

How have you used this book to help yourself or others?_____

_____

_____

_____

If you are interested in how we can help you or your organization with workshops, seminars, retreats or executive coaching on workplace change-loss grief, please send us the following information. Thanks for your feedback.

Name of person requesting information _____

Title _____

Organization _____

Address _____

City/State/Zip _____

Telephone _____ FAX _____

John S. Jeffreys, Ed.D. & Associates
410/730-6070
FAX 310/854–0413

OVER 150 BOOKS AND 35 VIDEOS AVAILABLE IN THE 50-MINUTE SERIES

We hope you enjoyed this book. If so, we have good news for you. This title is part of the best-selling *50-MINUTE™ Series* of books. All *Series* books are similar in size and identical in price. Many are supported with training videos.

To order *50-MINUTE* Books and Videos or request a free catalog, contact your local distributor or Crisp Publications, Inc., 1200 Hamilton Court, Menlo Park, CA 94025. Our toll-free number is (800) 442-7477.

50-Minute Series Books and Videos Subject Areas . . .

Management
Training
Human Resources
Customer Service and Sales Training
Communications
Small Business and Financial Planning
Creativity
Personal Development
Wellness
Adult Literacy and Learning
Career, Retirement and Life Planning

Other titles available from Crisp Publications in these categories

Crisp Computer Series
The Crisp Small Business & Entrepreneurship Series
Quick Read Series
Management
Personal Development
Retirement Planning